A STEP-BY-STEP BOOK ABOUT
DWARF HAMSTERS

CHRIS HENWOOD

Photography: All photos by Michael Gilroy, except as otherwise noted.

Humourous drawings by Andrew Prendimano.

9 8 7 6 5 4 3 2 1   **1996 Edition**   9 6 7 8 9

Distributed in the UNITED STATES to the Pet Trade by T.F.H. Publications, Inc., One T.F.H. Plaza, Neptune City, NJ 07753; distributed in the UNITED STATES to the Bookstore and Library Trade by National Book Network, Inc. 4720 Boston Way, Lanham MD 20706; in CANADA to the Pet Trade by H & L Pet Supplies Inc., 27 Kingston Crescent, Kitchener, Ontario N2B 2T6; Rolf C. Hagen Ltd., 3225 Sartelon Street, Montreal 382 Quebec; in CANADA to the Book Trade by Vanwell Publishing Ltd., 1 Northrup Crescent, St. Catharines, Ontario L2M 6P5 ; in ENGLAND by T.F.H. Publications, PO Box 15, Waterlooville PO7 6BQ; in AUSTRALIA AND THE SOUTH PACIFIC by T.F.H. (Australia), Pty. Ltd., Box 149, Brookvale 2100 N.S.W., Australia; in NEW ZEALAND by Brooklands Aquarium Ltd. 5 McGiven Drive, New Plymouth, RD1 New Zealand; in Japan by T.F.H. Publications, Japan—Jiro Tsuda, 10-12-3 Ohjidai, Sakura, Chiba 285, Japan; in SOUTH AFRICA by Lopis (Pty) Ltd., P.O. Box 39127, Booysens, 2016, Johannesburg, South Africa. Published by T.F.H. Publications, Inc.

MANUFACTURED IN THE UNITED STATES OF AMERICA
BY T.F.H. PUBLICATIONS, INC.

Contents

The whole idea and aim of this book is really to help you to decide if the Russian and/or Chinese Hamsters will make suitable pets for you and, if so, how to look after them. It will also, I hope, tell you as much as you will need to know should you decide to actually own some.

INTRODUCTION

With this in mind first, I would ask you to please read this book from cover to cover BEFORE you go out and buy your animals. Then answer the following questions: (1) Can I house and look after these little animals in the way they should be looked after? (2) Do I have sufficient time to care for them? (3) Do I really want a pet at all? (4) Do other members of the household feel positive about my having these pets?

If ANY of these questions is answered in the negative, then, be honest with yourself and for the sake of the animals reconsider your decision to engage in this hobby. If you answered "yes" to all of the questions, then I hope that you enjoy whichever of the various species of Dwarf Hamster you decide to have. May they give you as much fun and happiness as I have been given by mine over the years.

Facing Page: Dwarf Hamsters, like all other animals, have specific needs and requirements that must be fulfilled if the pet-to-person relationship is to be a happy and rewarding one.

DWARF HAMSTERS

There are at least 24 different species or subspecies of hamster distributed throughout Africa and Eurasia, as far east as China. However, in this book I shall be dealing with basically four species or subspecies, which are known collectively as the Dwarf Hamsters. Although to be totally correct they actually comprise two different groups: one the "true" Dwarf Hamsters, the other a member of the so-called "Rat-like" Hamsters. They are the Russian and Chinese Hamsters respectively.

Twenty years ago if you had mentioned either of these hamster-types, I doubt that many people would have been able to tell you what they looked like, let alone where they could be obtained. Now they are quite commonplace pets in the UK and Europe and are being imported into the USA. They are approximately half the size of the normally seen Golden or Syrian Hamster. Why these Dwarf species have suddenly gained popularity as pets I cannot say. It could be that they are smaller and undoubtedly have great charm, that they can be retained in pairs, small family groups and in some circumstances colonies, unlike Golden Hamsters. Or very simply it could be that they are becoming more easily obtainable.

Many "authorities" will tell you that Russian Hamsters will live most happily in colonies. I personally find that they are best in pairs, either of the same or opposite sex. This fact holds true for all species in this book.

A breeding pair that has had a litter left with it may refuse to breed again until the litter is removed. But this is certainly not always the case. I have had pairs that have produced a litter even before the previous litter had been properly weaned. The males make extremely good fathers if they are given the chance by the female, helping with the nest building and keeping the young warm while the female is feeding; although, as with all aspects of life, it does depend on each individual animal.

Dwarf Hamsters are climbing the ladder of popularity with pet owners. Besides their relative smallness, these Hamsters have many endearing qualities that make them very attractive as pets.

Chinese Hamsters are not all that different really. They can be rather quarrelsome amongst themselves. The females are particularly prone to nibbling and biting the male's tail and genital region. However, I have found that over recent years this has become less and less common and is virtually unknown in the strain containing the Dominant Spot genes.

The major problem with both the Russian and Chinese is, if one of a pair dies, it is often very difficult to pair any adult individual with another. But, having said this, it can be done. But actually giving any hard or fast rules on how, I am afraid is quite impossible. What may work with one pair may not with another. You need to know your animals, particularly the temperament of each. Males tend to accept a younger female much more readily than a female will accept a young male. The exception to this is if by chance the female still has a litter with her on the death of the male. You can then often leave a son in with his mother.

THE DWARF RUSSIAN HAMSTER

There are three species of Dwarf Russian Hamster. Although some authorities feel that they should be regarded as subspecies, I tend to believe, from the evidence of breeding in captivity, that they should be regarded as separate species.

Campbell's Dwarf Russian Hamster — *Phodopus sungoris campbelli*

This is the most commonly retained and seen of the different Russians. It is also known as the Original, Djungarian, Striped or Furry Footed Dwarf Russian Hamster. But I prefer the name Campbell's, and it is by this name that I shall refer to this species throughout this book.

They are found in the wild throughout Kazah and Mongolia, although the main population centre appears to be the Djungarian region of Mongolia. In size, this species is approximately 8 cms in length, with a short tail that is usually hidden by its thick fur. The female is slightly smaller than the male. The coat colour is brownish grey/beige, often being more beige in the winter than the summer. There is a conspicuous yet quite fine blackish brown dorsal stripe from between the ears to the base of the tail, although in some individuals this stripe fades out over the rump. The belly fur is a buffish white.

There a mutation available in the UK, with a few individuals having been exported to Sweden in 1985 and beginning to establish themselves there. This is a satin coated variety. It has a recessive gene which to some extent thins and darkens the coat colour. It was discovered in stock originally from the Zoological Society of London by Peter and Doreen Marsh of Maidstone, Kent, England in 1981. After much work and outcrossing the satin gene was established and introduced to the pet market in the

Introduced to the pet market in 1978, Winter White Dwarf Russian Hamsters have found many a happy home with pet owners on both sides of the Atlantic.

UK by my wife and me in 1985. The satin gene is a little more difficult to breed, as both parents must be either satin coated individuals or carry this gene to produce satin coated offspring.

Little is certain about the introduction of this species into the UK. It is likely that the first introduction was in 1963 by the Zoological Society of London, although it was not bred successfully in any numbers until 1968. It was introduced onto the pet market from stock obtained by Mr. Percy Parslow from the ZSL in approximately 1975, yet it was not until the early 1980's that this species became widely available.

Winter White Dwarf Russian Hamster - *Phodopus sungoris sungoris*

There is really no "official" common name for this species; the name "Winter White" was adopted in the late 1970's to describe it, due to the fact that the coat may turn completely white when the individual animal is subjected to the winter day length, namely 16 hours of dark and 8 hours of light even in captivity. Some so-called authorities object to this name but they have yet to propose any other name; therefore, it is this name that I shall be using here.

This species originates in the wild from Siberia and Manchuria. It is slightly larger than Campbell's, with slightly thicker fur. The eyes are larger and the ears less conspicuous. The overall colour is darker, being more greyish black than beige, the belly colour tends to be more whitish than any of the other Dwarf species.

The Winter White was introduced into the UK in the 1970's as a laboratory animal. It was introduced onto the pet market by me in 1978 from stock obtained from the now non-existent colony at Queen Mary's College, London.

The subspecies *Phodopus sungoris sungoris* is also known as the Winter White. Note the size of the eyes and ears and the colouration of the coat.

It may be hard to imagine how immense we must seem to these Dwarf Russian Hamsters—three of whom fit comfortably in the palm of our hand.

Raborovski's Dwarf Russian Hamster - *Phodopus raborovski*

Known quite simply as Raborovski's Hamster, this species is found in the wild in western and southern Mongolia and the adjacent parts of Manchuria and northern China.

In appearance it is similar to Campbell's but has much longer legs and bigger, more noticeable rounded ears. In habits, it is very similar to the other Dwarf Russian Hamsters and may be treated in the same general manner.

11

SHOW STANDARDS

Over the past few years the keeping of the Dwarf Russian Hamster and the Chinese Hamster has increased so much that people have begun to wish to show these species in the same ways as their larger cousin, the Syrian Hamster. Therefore in 1986 I, along with members of what has now become GOSH (The Group for Other Species of Hamsters), established standards for these species. They are as follows:

Dwarf Russian Hamster - Campbell's Normal Coated

1. COLOUR

The top colour shall be a brownish buffish grey to ochre grey, with a slate blue undercoat. The belly fur should be whitish with a heavy blue-grey undercolour. The feet are haired and white.

2. TYPE AND BUILD

The build should be likened to a bullet, roundish in shape. The legs should be short. The tail very short and scarcely visible.

3. FUR

The fur to be dense with a very thick undercoat. The entire coat and undercoat to give a woolly impression.

4. HEAD, EYES, EARS AND LEGS

The head to be short and broad with noticeable cheeks. The round eyes must not bulge; black in colour. The ears are small and round yet show above the fur, the insides to be a little hairy. The soles of the hind feet shall be covered in dense fur.

5. SIZE

An adult shall have an ideal length of approximately 7 cms.

6. MARKINGS

The boundary between the belly and top colour is formed by three prominently marked arches. The colour of the arches is dark buff to black. A dark black-brown stripe runs from between the eyes, down the back to the base of the tail.

7. CONDITION

The hamster must show a lively image with clear bright eyes.

This Dwarf Hamster is known as Campbell's Normal Coated. The dedicated efforts of the author, members of GOSH, and others have contributed to their popularity and helped to establish fixed and reliable type. Photo by Chris Henwood.

8. MINOR FAULTS

Small deviation in type, build and size. Slight moulting and colour deviation. Thin fur and short stripe.

9. MAJOR FAULTS

Large deviations in type, build and size. Heavy moulting and thin fur. Partial or total lack of stripe. Sick, bald, wounded or pregnant individuals. Any animal that refuses to be handled or bites.

Campbell's Satin Coated

The standard for the satin coated animal should be the same as that for the normal coated animals, allowing for the satinisation of the coat which darkens the colours. The fur shall be extremely fine and glossy giving a somewhat less dense appearance.

Points for both varieties of Campbell's:

Colour	25
Type and Build	15
Fur	15
Head, Eyes, Ears and Legs	15
Size	10
Markings	10
Condition	10
Total	100
Minor Faults	-10 max
Major Faults	-20 max

Introduction

Campbell's Satin Coated Hamster. **Photo by Chris Henwood.**

Dwarf Russian Hamster - Winter White

1. COLOUR

The top colour shall be a grey-brown to ochre grey, with a slate blue undercoat. The belly fur must be a clean white, the undercoat may be slightly tinged with a little blue. The feet are white.

N.B. With winter day length the colour moults to a complete white, with the exception of the dorsal stripe. A show animal should not show signs of this moult, unless a special class has been established for this situation.

2. TYPE AND BUILD

The build should be likened to a bullet, roundish in shape. The legs should be short. The tail very short and scarcely visible.

The summer and winter coats of the Winter White. The Hamster with the darker colouration sports the summer coat, while the lighter coloured Hamster displays the winter coat. Photo by Chris Henwood.

3. FUR

The fur to be dense with a very thick undercoat. The entire coat to give a woolly impression.

4. HEAD, EYES, EARS AND LEGS

The head to be short and broad with noticeable cheeks. The round eyes must not bulge; black in colour. The ears are small, rounded, and the inside to be a little hairy. The soles of the hind feet shall have dense fur.

5. SIZE

An adult shall have an ideal length of approximately 7 cms.

6. MARKINGS

The boundary between the belly and top colour is formed

by three prominently marked arches. The colour of the arches is dark brown to black fading to light brown or grey. A dark black-brown stripe runs from between the eyes, down the back to the base of the tail.

7. CONDITION

The hamster must show a lively image with clear bright eyes.

8. MINOR FAULTS

As for Campbell's Normal Coated.

9. MAJOR FAULTS

As for Campbell's Normal Coated.

Points as for Campbell's Normal Coated.

Chinese Hamster - *Cricetulus griseus*

Not strictly a Dwarf Hamster, but in fact a "Rat-like" Hamster. The Chinese Hamster has had a rather up and down history in the UK and I for one am not sure why—probably due to the fact that it used to be very difficult to breed. At times it has been very popular and has then fallen from grace. It has been retained in the UK at least since 1919, although mainly in laboratories. It has been stated that the difficulty in breeding this species accounted for the search for a new species and the discovery of the Syrian Hamster in 1930.

The original stocks are thought to have originated from various wild captures in Mongolia, China and Manchuria; however, the particular stock from which animals in the UK are thought to descend from are assumed to be those captured just outside Peking in 1925.

This species of "Rat-like" Hamster is one of the

smallest; in size adult males are approximately 9-10 cms long. They are rather long and thin in general appearance, males appearing much longer than the females because of their extended scrotum. The reason for this rather large scrotal sac is thought to be so that the testes drag slightly on the floor of their tunnel homes and thereby lower the temperature of the semen.

In colour the "normal" Chinese is a greyish brown, with a conspicuous blackish brown dorsal stripe from between the eyes to the base of the tail; the belly is whitish. Juveniles tend to be rather greyer than the adults.

In 1981–82 a mutation of this species occurred at the British University of Birmingham, creating an almost totally white individual. This animal was dark eyed and therefore not an albino. When mated to a normal individual it produced a number of young, all normal coloured but with varying amounts of white spots and patches— not one single all-white youngster. Since this point, with selective breeding, many white-spotted young have been produced, yet only a few all-white individuals and of these very few have been fertile; and those that I have known have not produced any all-white young. All tend to be slightly smaller and have a shorter life span than the normal or spotted animals. This white spotting was discovered to be a dominant gene and was introduced to the pet market by me in 1984 and has, I believe, been responsible for the renewed interest in this species.

GOSH Standards for the Chinese Hamster - Normal Coloured

1. COLOUR

The top colour shall be brownish grey to yellowish ochre, with a dark slate blue base colour. The belly fur shall be beige/white with a dark blue base colour.

Introduction

Note the short dense fur, the clear round eyes, and the small rounded ears of this Chinese Hamster.

2. TYPE AND BUILD

The build should be long and slender. The legs should be short and the tail long.

3. FUR

The fur to be short and dense.

4. HEAD, EYES, EARS AND LEGS

The head to be as triangular as possible. The round eyes must not over-bulge; black in colour. The ears are small and rounded; blackish brown in colour, the rim of the ears shall be a light coloured cream white. The feet are haired and white in colour; the nails should be neutral.

5. SIZE

An adult should ideally be approximately 3-4 ins (7.6-10.2 cms).

6. MARKINGS

Between back and belly colour there shall be a well-defined straight line from the nose, over the cheeks, and along the sides. The dorsal stripe shall be regular from between the eyes to the base of the tail.

7. CONDITION

The hamster must show a lively image with clear, bright eyes.

Many Dwarf Hamsters can be kept in mixed-sex pairs. Remember, however, that pregnancy is deemed a major fault in the show circle. Photo by Chris Henwood.

Exercise is important for health and happiness in your Dwarf Hamster. Whether your Hamster is to be a show winner or solely a pet, give it plenty of opportunity to stretch and work its muscles.

8. MINOR FAULTS

Small deviation in type, build and size. Slight moulting and colour deviation. Thin fur and short stripe.

9. MAJOR FAULTS

Large deviation in type, build and size. Heavy moulting and patchy fur. Partial or total lack of stripe. Sick, bald, wounded, badly scared or pregnant animals. Animals that refuse to be handled or bite.

Dominant Spot Variety

1. COLOUR

The top colour shall be a brownish grey to yellowish ochre with dark slate blue base colour. Both top and base

colour may be broken by a varying amount of white spots or patches. The distribution of these white areas should be as even as possible. The belly fur shall be a clean crisp white.

2. Type and Build

The build should be long and slender. The legs should be short, the tail long.

3. Fur

The fur to be short and dense.

4. Head, Eyes, Ears and Legs

Head to be triangular as possible. The round eyes must not over-bulge; black in colour. The ears are small and rounded; blackish brown in colour, with or without light coloured patches. The rim of the ears shall be light coloured cream to white. The feet are haired and white in colour; the nails should be neutral.

5. Size

An adult should have an ideal size of approximately 3-4 ins (7.6-10.2 cms).

6. Markings

Between the back and belly colour there shall be a well-defined straight line from the nose over the cheeks and along the sides. This stripe may be broken by the white areas. The Dorsal stripe which runs from the eyes to the base of the tail may also be broken by white spots or patches.

7. Condition

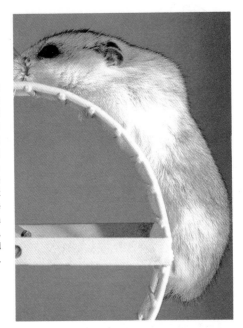

Persistence and dedication are two qualities found in the Dwarf Hamster. Faced with a challenge, they will work to rise above it. Pet owners too should practice these qualities, for Dwarf Hamsters are relatively new to the pet market and we may have to work to keep them growing in soundness, health, and good disposition.

The hamster must show a lively image with clear bright eyes.

8. MINOR FAULTS

As for the Normal Coloured Chinese.

9. MAJOR FAULTS

As for the Normal Coloured Chinese.

Points for both varieties of Chinese Hamster:

Colour	25
Type and Build	15
Fur	15
Head, Eyes, Ears and Legs	15
Size	10
Markings	10
Condition	10
Total	100
Minor Faults	-10 max
Major Faults	-20 max

D ue to their short-sightedness, hamsters of all species get to know their owners mainly by smell and sound. An important part of getting to know your pets is to speak to them at feeding times. This should usually be in the early evening.

HANDLING AND TAMING

Having placed the day's supply of food into the cage, tap gently on the side of the cage to wake up the hamsters if they are not already awake. On no account poke your finger into the nest to wake them up, as this will startle them and they are then likely to bite. I found this out once to my cost when I poked my finger into the nest of a pair of Campbell's Russians that I regarded as the most friendly that I owned; however, I received a very nasty bite not from the adults but from a two-day-old baby that I didn't know had been born. Anyone who tells you a hamster without its eyes open can't bite, doesn't know hamsters. I still have the scar to prove it.

Handle your animals one at a time. When the hamster comes out and begins to investigate the food, very gently stroke it, talking to it all the time. At first it may flinch or even run back to its nest, but don't let this deter you; it will soon get used to you and sit quite still while you stroke it.

Facing Page: Handling and taming require patience and delicacy. Handle your Hamsters one at a time with gentle strokes and slow movements.

Do not, at this point, attempt to pick it up or grab at it. Avoid making any loud noises or rapid movements; do not move your hands in a swooping movement towards the back of the animal, since this is the direction from which most predators strike. Such movements may cause the animal to bite first and see whom it is biting second. Be patient. Stroke the hamster when it comes out for food for the next two or three nights. Then, offer a tidbit, such as a small piece of apple or carrot or sweet dry biscuit, so that it will get used to receiving special foods from your fingers, which, don't forget, are huge great things to such a small creature. Obtain a small piece of stiff wire mesh and coax one of the hamsters onto it. Take your time and concern yourself with one animal at a time. Once on the mesh, stroke it gently while talking to it and then return it to the cage with a tidbit. Again, repeat this with each animal for several nights, gradually closing your hand over the hamster. Within a few days, you should be able to pick it up off the wire and put it back into its cage; naturally, some will take to being handled more quickly than others.

Early handling usually results in well tamed adults. This photo is of a Winter White at 10 days of age.

To some, handling a tamed Hamster is one of the most enjoyable aspects of the hobby. If your Hamster was reared properly, there should be no problem in handling him at any age.

You may find that the best way of handling each animal is to cup your whole hand over it. Be careful that you do not squeeze it as this will make it bite. Unlike the case with its big cousin, it is often difficult to scruff a Dwarf as it is much more liable to turn in its own skin and bite you.

I personally have never had any problems with handling Chinese Hamsters; although they can be jumpy and must be calmed down, they rarely bite. Be warned—they do have another way of putting you off; they often urinate all over a strange person, as many a judge has found out to his or her cost.

When buying a hamster of any species, please do not attempt to try to look around for bargains or the cheapest animals; good animals, even breeding pairs of unusual varieties, are not expensive.

The best-aged hamster to buy is between five and twelve weeks of age, particularly a single sexed pair for

SELECTION

pets. Those only or primarily for breeding may be a little bit older but not more than twenty-four weeks.

All baby hamsters of whatever species are shy and can be easily frightened, so it is useless to attempt to tame a baby too early.

Pet shops on the whole vary in the way they keep and display hamsters. Up to eight or ten weeks of age it really doesn't matter if they are retained in single or mixed sexed groups. Between ten and sixteen weeks females from a mixed group may be pregnant; therefore, if you do not wish to breed, it would probably be better to obtain males only. Naturally, if you wish to breed, this doesn't matter, although you will not know which male is the father of the litter.

Always avoid anyone selling hamsters who refuses to handle them for you. It is often these animals that bite and will therefore not only make unsuitable pets but may pass this trait on to their offspring as well.

Facing Page: This photo shows a Chinese and a Winter White. They should not be kept together in the same housing unit.

The best way to handle all new smaller hamsters is to cup them between both your hands, thus preventing the animal from jumping into the air. Hamsters have little ideas as to height.

Always inspect your chosen animal for sores or large wounds. If it has any, refuse it. Some scars may occur, particularly if the hamster is obtained direct from a breeding colony. But these should be well healed, not open or infected.

Before selecting your Hamster, observe it in its home. Watch for any unusual behavior and look closely for any signs of illness.

Many people believe that the eyes are good indicators of the health of the animal. When observing your potential pet, check for clear, bright, alert eyes. Check also for discharge from the eyes, as this could indicate a health problem.

Hamsters, including those in this book, will survive on almost any diet. This does not mean, however, that they will be either happy or healthy on any old food. The basic diet as with all rodents is, to a lesser or greater extent, the same, normally being made up of various seeds and cereals and vegetable matter when available.

FEEDING

As you will be aware if you have kept any pet, if food is obtained in bulk, it will work out much cheaper. Usually you can buy either a ready made mixture in a single large bag, or, if you wish, more smaller bags of various foods to mix together yourself. Should you decide on the former, the best mix is that commonly known as Hamster Mix. However, whichever you decide upon you will find that the following are most commonly involved:

Oats

Often the basis of the entire diet is oats. They may be obtained in several forms: whole, crushed or clipped. Although there is a large amount of waste when using crushed oats, where any hamster is concerned I would advise using this rather than whole or clipped oats as the sharp husks of the oats may well harm the delicate lining of the pouches and cause abscess.

Facing Page: Success in feeding has been found in using a proven base food such as wheat or oats supplemented with a variety of other quality foods.

Wheat

Along with oats, this can be used as a basic food-stuff, often in equal parts with oats. Wheat is very rich in Vitamin E and is said to greatly assist fertility. However, if too much wheat is used in the diet, it will often be left by the animals and therefore go to waste.

Maize

This is basically corn and, like oats, may be obtained in a number of different forms, the most common being flaked or clipped; both are useful in the diet, but should be included only in small amounts as it is a heating food and may cause individual animals to scratch and cause open wounds on their skin. One advantage to this food is that the whole seed is eaten and therefore there is very little waste.

Maize as a feed is useful and economical. However, it must be fed only in small amounts, as maize is a "heating" food and too much can cause your Dwarf Hamster to scratch.

Chinese and Russian Hamsters become so engrossed in feeding that they can be gently scooped up and moved to a new location with little disturbance to them, so long as they have plenty of vittles to nibble along the way.

Pelleted Foods

Most commonly sold in pet stores as either rabbit, rat or cavy (guinea pig) pellets. Always avoid those that are sold only for commercial rabbit production as they usually have a drug added that is very helpful to rabbits but can be harmful to rodents.

Pelleted foods are a compounded food and contain a balanced amount of foods and vitamins. These pellets are a useful part of the diet, but they should not be regarded as a complete diet on their own, particularly for Russian Hamsters.

You can grow your own greens for your Dwarf Hamster. Pet shops sell greenhouse kits that provide everything you need to grow fresh organic greens. Photo courtesy of Four Paws.

Sunflower Seeds

These seeds are relished by all rodents. They are rich in Vitamin E and oil. Often, if allowed, individual animals will greatly overeat and cause themselves damage by becoming overweight and in some cases too hot. Therefore, only a small proportion of any mix should be made up of this item.

Peanuts

As with sunflowers, peanuts are a favourite food and also have their drawbacks. One particular side effect is that if overfed to hamsters they often make the individuals smell.

Feeding

Biscuits

Usually they are broken dog biscuits, but hard dried foods often have the appearance of biscuits. It doesn't really matter what type you use. They all form a useful food item, but are also important in that they give the animals something very hard on which to chew and thereby prevent their teeth from overgrowing.

Although the above is a basic diet, many items may be added to allow the individual animals variety. I add to my own mix dried vegetables, protein pellets and small seeds normally sold for finches and other small birds (these being useful for babies). Dwarf Hamsters appear on the whole to be much less interested in unusual foods than the Syrian Hamster.

Below are a few items that my own animals have liked over the years. You will undoubtedly find others.

You can add variety to your pet's diet by offering treats made especially for small animals like Dwarf Hamsters. Photo courtesy of Vitakraft.

One way to get an idea of your Hamster's favourite food is to scatter a wide variety and observe the order of consumption.

The only thing to be careful of is that any vegetable matter given has been washed to ensure that no trace of insecticide is on it, or, if you try wild berries or haws that they are not harmful to rodents in general.

Lettuce

Although this is a most popular item to give small pets, lettuce in excess can and does cause a rather dangerous liver complaint. But please don't misunderstand me; lettuce is a useful food, but in small amounts only.

Cabbage, etc.

This is a wide family of green vegetables but on the whole I have found that the flavour is too strong for my hamsters. The only variety they appear to like is curly kale. Again as with lettuce; small amounts only.

Root Crops

Again a very wide variety of items, by far the most liked and useful are carrots. They are seldom refused and on the whole can do no harm, although they may cause the urine to colour slightly.

Other items that may be taken by individuals are very varied but include: celery, apples, bean sprouts, sweet oranges, banana, avocado, pear and parsley, as well as a wide variety of different nuts. Small amounts of cooked meats such as chicken may be taken as will insects such as mealworms; but I would not regard this as part of the normal diet—just additional tidbits.

In cold weather, cold or warm mashes similar to those given to rabbits may be given, particularly if individuals are kept in a shed or outhouse. Mashes can be of items such as oat flakes, bran, barley, rice, lentils, etc.; but again it will depend on individuals' tastes and they should be given as an addition to the diet of seeds, not instead of it.

Dwarf Hamsters are hoarding animals. They will search out, find and store any excess food scattered about the cage.

HOUSING

Housing for Dwarf Hamsters comes in a wide variety of sizes, shapes, and constructions—from simple homes for a single pet to vast arrangements capable of containing large colonies. Housing purchased at your local pet shop is easy to use, economical and readily available. You may even find kits that include all the preliminary materials necessary for starting a successful hobby. It may also be possible for you to build a cage; but as a rule, buy, don't build. Anything you make can probably be bought for less.

Choose a cage as large as possible, at least one square foot. Hamsters pile up bedding material at one location and use another site to urinate and defecate, thus making it easy for you to clean the cage. As far as depth is concerned, two inches is minimal.

A ten gallon all-glass aquarium is ideal since most pet shops sell "leakers" very inexpensively, and the Dwarf Hamster does not care if the tank leaks water or not. If an aquarium is used, buy a fitted screen top or wire mesh cover that locks in place, allowing plenty of ventilation yet preventing a Dwarf Hamster from knocking the top off and escaping.

A Dwarf Hamster's home needs to be easily cleaned. Therefore, avoid cages made of wood. Although

Facing Page: Housing should be considered prior to purchase. Consider the space and finances available and the space and conditions necessary.

they may be cheaper than other cages, they are not always practical. The wood will soak up urine and will remain damp. Urine-soaked wood takes on a putrid odour and becomes a breeding ground for disease-causing germs. Cages made of plastic, glass, or stainless steel are all highly recommended. A plastic or metal cage is easily cleaned; it is also light enough to be transported and requires very little maintenance to keep it in good condition.

Furthermore, like all other rodents, Dwarf Hamsters like to gnaw, and it may not take long for your pet to chew through a wooden cage bottom. If the wood is splintery and sharp, it can hurt the Dwarf Hamster's mouth or cheek pouches. Metal cages are especially resistant to damage caused by gnawing, and many plastic cages can also withstand a Dwarf Hamster's constant gnawing.

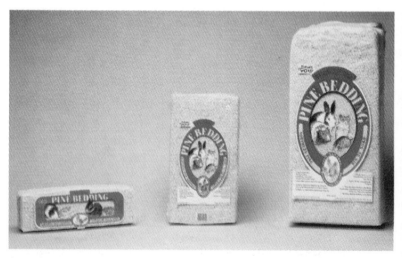

A good-quality bedding will absorb urine and help to mask any unpleasant odour that may be omitted. Because Dwarf Hamsters like to move the bedding around, the bottom of the cage should be covered with at least a two-inch layer of bedding. Photo courtesy of Hagen.

A Dwarf Hamster loves to roam freely. To accomplish this and still keep the animal contained there are various types of housing. Certain products allow you to build and design your Dwarf Hamster's housing in a number of ways. Photo courtesy of Hagen.

With some cages there is really no need for interior food containers, nor is it necessary to scatter food on the cage floor. A food hopper or feeding chute opening into the cage simplifies feeding and prevents a Dwarf Hamster from piling bedding material over the food or from soaking it with urine when the food is placed loosely in the cage. An interior water dish is to be avoided because your Dwarf Hamster will deliberately fill it with litter and wastes.

Access to water is best handled with an inexpensive, conventional water bottle that cannot be spilled or dirtied. This consists of a bottle containing a cork or rubber stopper with a metal, glass, or plastic drinking tube inserted into it. The bottle is hung upside down from the side or top of the cage by means of a clip. It should be positioned so water can be lapped from the tube while the animal is in a standing position. The end of the tube will probably be about one to two inches from the bottom of the cage. A bottle with a stainless steel drinking tube

Ladders, wheels, tunnels, and other accessories give your pets something to entertain themselves on, thus providing them with the exercise that is necessary for their good health.

is preferred because a Dwarf Hamster's constant gnawing can damage a plastic tube and crack a glass one.

Any cover should have a simple but strong latch that is easy to lock but not easy for your pet to unlock. Dwarf Hamsters are great escape artists. This cover should also provide good ventilation. A coarsely screened cover will be of interest to a Dwarf Hamster for exercise. Your pet will climb about upside down for many hours. The cover will also receive its share of gnawing, so be sure it is sufficiently strong.

A well stocked pet shop will have various toys to provide your pet with amusement. Do not use children's toys because Dwarf Hamsters chew on the plastic and it might be toxic if they swallow some. An exercise wheel is a great accessory if there is room for it in the cage. It does not really matter whether the wheel is a solid type or a spoked one, so long as the animal can comfortably work the wheel without any risk of injury.

A very useful accessory item is a plastic, glass, or metal scoop a bit larger than your Dwarf Hamster. There are times when it is more convenient to move Dwarf Hamsters in a container such as a retrieval before your pet Dwarf Hamster is tame or when cleaning the cage of a mother and her young. The scoop protects you from being bitten.

A large-mouthed glass jar, a round pound-sized rolled oats box, or a plastic bottle with the bottom removed are all excellent for transportation. Place a handful of food in the receptacle and scoop up the animal. While it is busy stuffing its pouches, the Dwarf Hamster can be moved anywhere.

Photo shows bite damage to a male's tail caused by an aggressive female.

Place plenty of litter or bedding in the cage to allow your Dwarf Hamster to move it around and create the desired terrain. A two- to three-inch layer of bedding is best. The bedding material can be nearly anything that is not poisonous, too aromatic, sharp or entangling. Cotton fibers tend to get caught in the Dwarf Hamster's feet, and sawdust is not very satisfactory as it can be easily thrown out of the cage and tends to pack down rather tightly when wet. Urine-soaked sawdust quickly becomes foul, and like a wooden cage bottom becomes a breeding ground for bacteria.

Spread lots of bedding over the bottom of the cage so the Dwarf Hamster can move it around to suit its needs; don't pile it up in one corner of the cage. Your Dwarf Hamster will hide food in certain areas, build its nest elsewhere, and sweep clean the spot where it leaves waste. This rearrangement creates another cage consideration. Some metal cages are constructed with a wire top and sides, with only a two-inch closed barrier along the bottom edges of the sides. As the Dwarf Hamsters move the material around, quite a bit of the bedding is scattered about the outside of the cage. Therefore, if a metal cage is used, it should have a solid back and sides, with a barrier across the front of at least three to four inches in height. Some cages come with a removable clear plastic barrier along the cage front. This allows you to see the Dwarf Hamster at all times and also keeps the litter in the cage.

Hamsters themselves have no external parasites, and with a little help from you, a weaned Dwarf Hamster will develop good toilet habits. The feces tend to dry out quickly and dry droppings are virtually odourless. However, the urine can present a problem. Clean the cage often enough to keep the urine spot localized. If the entire cage is dirty and damp, your pet has no reason to choose a particular place to wet. Hamsters tend to pile up bedding material at one site and use another location having a bare bottom for waste, making it easy for you to mop the wetness.

If using an open housing unit for your Dwarf Hamster it is important to keep a screen or cover on the enclosure to ensure the hamster's safety. Photo courtesy of Four Paws.

The floor litter needs to be removed entirely at weekly intervals and replaced with fresh litter. If you clean the cage too frequently, you may unsettle the Dwarf Hamster by disturbing its hoard too often.

Thorough cage cleaning is an essential part of your regular routine. Every few weeks wash the cage with hot, soapy water and a stiff brush. A mild disinfectant can be added, but do not use insect sprays or dusts since some may be lethal to your pet. By frequently pro-

viding fresh bedding, insects and their eggs will be entirely eliminated or kept well under control without the use of insecticides.

While the female is tending her litter, the owner must not disrupt the cage. Except for the solid corner, her cage should not be thoroughly cleaned until the cubs' eyes are open. The rest of the cage contents should be left alone. It is a good idea to provide plenty of extra bedding material during this period.

Without access to a wheel or other exercise accessories, your Dwarf Hamster may become sedentary and even discontented. With nothing to do all day, the naturally inquisitive Hamster could become a lethargic, uninteresting, unhealthy pet.

Housing

A well stocked pet shop will have many accessories that your pet will find entertaining. The inclusion of these affordable and available items could mean the difference between a well adjusted and a poorly dispositioned Dwarf Hamster.

If you expect to introduce additional Dwarf Hamsters to your stock, a cage should be kept empty and apart—preferably in another room—as quarantine for new or sick animals. Cages of sick Dwarf Hamsters require thorough washing and disinfecting before they are used again. The cage should have a private area for sleeping and hoarding, and enough space for a toilet area. You must provide water, adequate ventilation, and dry, warm cage litter. Hamsters ask for very little, just a simple diet and a draft-free cage. They are very fussy about their beds, and will spend a lot of time making a nest—only to move it if they feel a draft. Do not place the cage in direct sunlight or any other bright, glaring light.

Discontented Dwarf Hamsters are typically those that are crowded, deprived of privacy, not permitted to hoard, or abused by owners or cagemates. However, even a happy Dwarf Hamster will continually try to escape because of its natural curiosity.

ESCAPES AND RECAPTURES

Like the Syrian Hamster, the Dwarf appears to spend quite an amount of time plotting and trying to figure out a way to escape from the cage. It is therefore quite likely that at some point in time, one or both or even more animals in a cage will escape. There is not usually any cause for alarm, as unless the room is full of holes to the outside or under the floor, they won't go far and often will stay together. You can usually catch them quite easily. In fact, you may well only realise that they aren't in their cage when you catch sight of a little furry creature scurrying across the floor.

To catch your hamster, all you need is a few tasty tidbits, a bucket or a smooth metal waste paper bin and a few thickish books, bricks or such like. Place the bucket

"If there's a will, there's a way," and the Dwarf Hamster has no shortage of will. Despite all your efforts to keep the Hamster contented, it will continuously search for a way out of its cage. Don't take this to heart, however, for it is the Hamster's nature and not your provision that results in such attempts to escape.

The allure of food may be the most successful way to lure your escapee back to its cage. Dwarf Hamsters seem ever-hungry. They seem forever on the hunt for food. Setting a "trap" baited with food may well return to captivity a hamster on the loose.

on the floor with the hamster cage open nearby; naturally, this is only if all the animals have escaped. If not, leave the cage closed; this will encourage the animals to come to a familar smell and source of food. In the bottom of the bucket, place a nice deep layer of shavings and bedding plus a small amount of food. Pile the bricks and/or books beside the bucket so that they form a type of steps or ramp to the top of the bucket and leave it in place overnight. In the morning your escapees will be found asleep in the bottom of the bucket. If you by chance have only caught one, repeat it again the next night.

This chapter is concerned not only with the breeding of the various species in this book but also the development of the young. So many of these areas are similar to all the species that I shall deal with them as a whole rather than as individuals. Although where differences do occur they will naturally be mentioned.

BREEDING

Both the Dwarf Russian and the Chinese Hamsters tend on the whole to have a smaller individual litter size than the Syrian Hamster. The average of all species is four individuals, with the Chinese often reaching eight or nine and the Winter White Russian two.

Although in the wild all species are seasonal breeders, they tend to be able to breed throughout the year in captivity. The Chinese often stop when temperatures get too high in the summer months but breed quite well in the winter. The Russians may stop during various times of the year and this usually appears to be connected with humidity rather than temperature.

On the whole all species appear to be able to survive the cold much better than heat; and the Chinese have been known to breed very successfully at 15°C (59°F). The ideal temperature for breeding all species appears to be about 21°C (70°F.)

Facing Page: Dwarf Hamsters in the wild tend to be seasonal breeders. In captivity, because you can control the climate, Dwarf Hamsters can be made to breed all the year through—keeping in mind, however, the stress and fatigue placed on a breeding animal.

All can be maintained in pairs of either the same or mixed sex or colonies. However, should you wish to breed for coat or colour mutations, then you must breed in pairs only. This enables you to know for certain exactly which female has produced a litter, and which male is the sire—an impossible situation in a colony. I have personally found that in colonies of Chinese you will often have an aggressive dominant female that may well make life very uncomfortable for others in the colony, particularly males. She may castrate or even kill them. However, this occurs much more rarely when pairs are maintained. However, when it does occur in pairs the first sign that you know it is taking place is the death of the male. This is because he is less able to get away from her.

Another drawback in the colony system occasionally occurs with the Russians once a colony is established. Breeding suddenly stops for no apparent reason. This is probably due to natural selection, and even removing a pair for breeding elsewhere may not change the situation. Occasionally, adult females will steal each other's litters which can lead to fighting and also the death of the litter. This can be rectified by removing the mother of the litter, if known, and a young male and establishing a new pair or colony.

Given the chance by the females, males of all the species make extremely good fathers; so do not worry about his being present at the birth of the litter. Also do not make the mistake of removing him from the cage when the female has a litter, as she will probably never accept him back again and in fact may well kill him. The males help with nest building and keeping the young warm while the female is feeding away from the nest or on occasions they will bring food to the nest for both the mother and babies. I have known females to chase the male out of the nest only to have him return minutes later as soon as the female has moved away to feed. This male did nothing more than wash and sleep with the babies and was promptly driven away again as soon as the female returned.

Breeding

Gestation for all species ranges from 18 to 30 days, but the usual length of pregnancy is 21 days. Females will usually, but not always, remate within 24 hours of producing a litter, thus often producing two litters of young within a six-week period.

Most females will make a nest of some form. This usually consists of a basic floor of sawdust or shavings with shredded tissue or hay piled around with the babies left in a hollow in the centre. The nests of the Chinese are, particularly in the winter months, much more elaborate than those of the Russians. When the babies are left by the female they may be left open so that you can have a good look at them or the female may cover the nest with more material to hide them completely. Don't worry, this light covering will not hurt the young. Unless you know your animals very well, never disturb the nest of a female with young before they are 10-12 days old, particularly if it is a first litter as the female may well kill the babies or just abandon them. If a female spreads the litter around the cage in this early part of their life and they appear to be being ignored, the best way in which to return them to the nest area is to gently scoop them

Dwarf Hamsters are, by comparison to us, very small animals. The newborns then are necessarily extremely tiny creatures. This photo is of a five-day-old Winter White Hamster.

up with a teaspoon and place them back under or as near to the female as possible.

Females will often chase the male out of the nest for the first day or so of the life of the young and then allow him to return once the babies are bigger. Often this is the first sign that you will notice that a litter is born—the male not in his usual place.

At birth the babies are naked and blind, but they do have teeth and whiskers. The skin darkens at about three days and even at this stage the dorsal stripe is quite clearly visible. The actual fur appears at 6-8 days and the eyes open at 14 days, although solid food will be taken from 9 days. They tend to be independent between 18-21 days. All species are sexually mature by 60 days but some individuals may be capable of producing young at 30 days.

The life span of the different species varies from 18-24 months in the Campbell's to 36-48 months in the Chinese Hamster. The oldest individual I have known of any of these species was a male Chinese Hamster which reached the age of 58 months.

As you can see, Chinese and Russian Dwarf Hamsters are similar in size when adults.

Dwarf Hamsters in the wild go through a selective mating process. In captivity, it is usually you, the owner, who selects the mate. Therefore, some pairs that you choose will not mate simply because the two animals are for some reason incompatible. In these situations there is little for the owner to do other than separate the animals and try another pairing.

I usually separate the litter from the parents at approximately 30 days. Occasionally these litters have younger litters already in the nest and the adults have pushed the babies out of the original nest area. However, sometimes all the babies are sharing the same nest area. At 30 days it is still possible to mix individuals of different litters together to allow individuals to be paired for outcrossing and thus prevent inbreeding. I try to avoid inbreeding (i.e., brother to sister matings) unless I am trying to establish a particular strain, for example satin coat. The reason for this is that I have found that increased brother to sister matings for more than three generations tend to increase the amount of fighting and aggressiveness of the individuals both with each other and their human owners.

All Dwarfs and Chinese fight a little as this is part of their normal play and social behaviour and they will rough and tumble for a lot of the time that they are awake, particularly when young. This play should not be mistaken for serious fighting and should not be interfered with. Such interference may well end the bond between the individuals and thereby cause serious fighting.

Should you decide to breed for either show or particular colour, etc., the importance of keeping accurate and up-to-date records cannot be over emphasized.

By far the most simple and successful way of doing this is to give each individual or pair a card. This card can either be fixed to the cage or stored in an index box. On this you should record such information as the animal's name or number, its type, parents, grandparents, age, the date of all litters produced, the size of each litter and any unusual thing about its behaviour, etc.

Before we finish with breeding, I think I ought to say something about the death of a member of a pair. Usually, once established, a pair will not accept a strange animal of either sex and may well kill it. As the species

In the front of the photo is a rare, all-white Chinese Hamster. Behind it is a spotted variety. Photo by Chris Henwood.

Breeding

Handling Hamsters at an early age will help familiarize them with humans and make them tamer pets.

are bred for a longer and longer period in captivity this is likely to change; however, at present it is best to assume that should a member of a pair die then you have lost the breeding potential of this pair. There are exceptions to this. Should a male die and the female still have a litter in the nest or be pregnant, then it may be possible to leave with her a son from one of these litters. On occasion, successful pairing may well occur if you have young individuals that have lost partners. Introduce them together on neutral territory, for example, a new cage. Disguise the smell of each animal from the other by perhaps spraying each of them with a smell that neither will recognise, for example deodorant spray that can be obtained from most pet shops. Always watch the individuals very carefully as fighting will usually occur quite quickly if it is going to. When they decide to settle down and sleep together you can usually assume that they have accepted each other. I have found over the last year or so that Chinese are much easier to pair together with strange animals than are Russians; however, whether this is just the strain of animals, I cannot say.

HEALTH

On the whole, all the smaller species of hamster are rather healthy individuals, with little disease occurring at all. Often when problems do arise it is so sudden that little can be done to help at all. With any serious ailment or in any case when you are not 100% sure what is wrong always contact your local Vet.

There are, however, some minor ailments that may occur that you should be able to recognise and cope with quite easily. First, let me mention one or two things that may occur and that even your Vet will not be able to help with. In these cases, it is usually safer and kinder to have your animal put to sleep by the Vet.

The Chinese Hamster on occasion develops a form of eye disorder. This appears to be hereditary and individuals showing this should not be used for breeding. These animals will usually show large, sore areas around the eyes which also appear watery, slightly opaque and very reddish. It is thought by some that this may also be the sign of kidney problems, but I cannot make any comment on this. The second and even rarer disease that occurs in the Chinese is a type of wasting disease, somewhat resembling the human form of muscular dystrophy. Both these diseases appear eventually to be fatal.

Occasionally Russian Hamsters, particularly the

Facing Page: Keeping a well bred Dwarf Hamster healthy is not hard to do. Hamsters are, for the most part, hardy creatures that require little work on the part of the owner to keep their health sound. As with all other animal species kept under conditions of captivity, however, occasional problems will occur.

Campbell's, develop what can only be described as ear warts. They occur only on the ear opening of adult animals and are not curable. They may grow very large and prevent hearing at which point it is sometimes possible to have them surgically removed. They appear to be caused by acute inbreeding and I would advise not breeding from stock showing this or, if you have already done so, outcrossing to another line with the very next generation.

The majority of the minor ailments that occur with hamsters are usually injuries caused by fighting. On the whole they are not too serious and can therefore be treated by applying one of the various wound dressing powders or creams obtainable from your Vet or pet shop. Occasionally a young female may remove the foot of a baby when it is very young and by the time you realise this the baby is moving about the cage quite happily on three legs and a stump. Provided this missing foot is a rear one, the individual should have no problem living a full and happy life. However, if it should be a front foot you will have to watch carefully that the hamster can feed itself properly and, if not, you may have to have the Vet put it to sleep.

Constipation can often be caused by unsuitable bedding such as cotton wool, wood wool, kapok or newspaper. Naturally, all bedding should be replaced with good meadow hay and fresh green foods should be given in larger amounts than normal. Should the condition not be cleared up within 24 hours then a Vet should be consulted. The opposite, diarrhea, may also occur and is nearly always caused by overfeeding green vegetables.

On rare occasions, Dwarf Hamsters develop infestations of mites. This appears to arise from infested hay or sawdust and once present can cause great problems. The usual signs of this are loss of fur and slight open sores. I have managed to rid stock of such infestations by using anti-mite sprays of the type sold for use on caged birds. Please do not use the types sold for fleas on cats and dogs as they are too strong for these small hamsters and could actually lead to their death.

The following books by T.F.H. Publications are available at pet shops everywhere.

SUGGESTED READING

TEDDY BEAR HAMSTERS
By Mervin F. Roberts
ISBN 0-87666-776-0
TFH PS-710
Contents: Hamster Facts. Classification And Useful Tables. Hamster Features. You And Your Pet. Choosing A Pet Hamster. Caging. Feeding. Children And Hamsters. Grooming And Bathing. Breeding. Raising Young Hamsters. Genetics. Genetics Glossary. Diseases.
Hard cover, 5½ x 8″, 96 pages, 46 black and white photos, 37 colour photos.

HAMSTERS: A Complete Introduction
By Mervin Roberts
Hardcvr. **CO-020 ISBN 0-86622-269-3**
Softcvr. **CO-020S ISBN 0-86622-282-0**
Audience: Author Roberts concentrates on providing the type of bedrock information that has its greatest value to beginners because it really explains *why* a hamster owner should do what he recommends.
5½ x 8½, 96 pages. Contains 98 full-colour photos and 5 full-colour line drawings.

HAMSTERS—KW-015
By Percy Parslow
ISBN 0-86622-831-4
Hard cover, with *protective vinyl jacket.* 5½ × 8″, completely illustrated with full-colour photos and drawings. 128 pages.

Index